Living Poetry for Today

Heartfelt poems tied to inspirational stories about love, loss, challenges, and money

Michael P. Lyons

Contents

Love Poems

The love of my life

Words Fail to Express Love

Words have not the power

To speak the feeling of love.

Love lies buried in our soul

The ink attempts to compose.

The Kiss

The universe kisses our galaxy.

The galaxy kisses our planet.

The sun and moon kisses Earth.

Our kisses toast love and fidelity.

The rain kisses the rivers

The rivers kiss the ocean.

The oceans kiss the land.

Our kisses toast hereafter eternal love.

Your kisses will remain with me forever

even when you're gone.

The Pledge

I make a promise to you I can keep.

As the sun rises and sets,

my love for you will go on and on.

Bound forever even when you're gone,

my love for you goes on and on.

We'll be together in heaven at the rising of dawn.

Our love goes on and on,

Forever, forever, forever bound.

A Real Man

A real man is one who

Helps others going through tough times,

Offers kindness,

Opens and holds doors.

A real man is one who cries without shame,

Appreciates the arts,

Feels nature and GOD in his soul,

And cares and loves his spouse and offspring

till death do they part.

I Believe in Love

I believe in love,

Love is life and life is love.

Love prefers others before oneself.

Love lives on after death.

To love others, one needs to love oneself.

Love unites two as one.

True love is more than physical, It's emotionally unconditional.

Love is a feeling of deep affection, fondness,

Tenderness, warmth, and intimacy.

Men and women's destiny is to love,

Men and women love being in love.

Love makes everything better.

Food tastes better, sunsets are prettier, life is better

When you're together.

Not believing in love makes you feel lonely, incomplete,

And forsaken.

Love moves mountains and conquers all; love heals all.

I believe in the power of love.

What Is Love?

Love is not:

A crush or lust,

Subordinating one's dreams and goals,

Serving others that don't please you.

True love is:

A feeling words fail to express,

Effortless,

Driven by the heart and soul,

Caring passionately about one and other,

The feeling you'd climb any mountain, swim any ocean

To be with your lover,

Adoring one another with your eyes,

Yearning and obsessing over one another,

Ascending physical attraction,

Loss of appetite when you're with your lover,

A feeling of nirvana.

Being in love is two people coming together as one

And forming a lifetime partnership.

Wedding Vows

Love resides in our hearts, so a wedding is proclaimed.

Expressing love without end.

So, what's the reason for becoming husband and wife?

It's offering up your heart and soul.

It's committing to pairing for life.

It is love.

It triggers a man to leave his friends.

Causes a woman to leave her home.

Emerging together as one.

It is love.

A woman draws life from her man,

Creating new life yet again.

It is love.

A man gains purpose for his life,

Protecting and providing for his family's fledging life.

It is love.

The marriage of your spirit causes both of you to go forth.

For better, for worse, for richer, for poorer,

In sickness and in health,

Until death do you part.

It is love.

Love versus Hurt

Falling out of love is too painful for me,

I've loved enough men to satisfy me.

All my love affairs began blissfully,

Ending with my man committing adultery.

My past love affair has unsettled me.

Was I to blame? Should I forgive?

My mind a mess and anger smolders within.

Years of counseling and living alone

Has given back peace of mind.

The hurt remains and won't go away.

I desire male companionship but I'm still too afraid.

Men and women are created to be together.

But the hurt remains and won't go away?

Years have now passed.

I still desire a man.

But he must be the right man.

So, I reach out to men.

Guarding and protecting my emotions within.

But I can't let loose as hard as I try.

I want to be loved but passing on love is a dilemma within.

So, what do I do in this mental state?

I'll keep looking for love,

Until my emotions tell me it's too late.

At some point in time,

I may find love isn't for me.

And living alone may satisfy me.

Nothing Will Keep Us from Being Together

I'm so thrilled I found you!

We now have each other.

Put your hand in my hand,

We're here for each other.

We'll do whatsoever to stay together.

Put your arms around me, embrace me.

You are much too good to be true.

I'll never leave you.

I'm so lucky I found you,

All I want to do is love you.

We'll build a life together.

Through good times and bad times,

We'll stand unruffled together.

When it's time to expire,

We'll be entombed together.

Death will not keep us from being together.

Pairing

I've said it before, I'll say it again,

I want to be more than your friend.

When I'm with you, you make me glow.

I love your smile along with your style.

There's nothing about you I don't like.

I can't continue being friends.

I love you.

And I promise to love you to the end.

I can't carry on loving you

If you don't feel the same.

So please make up your mind,

I can't continue just being friends.

My love is on the line,

And there comes a time,

When a commitment must be made.

So, cut me free or commit to loving me,

For I can't go on loving thee in solitary.

If you cut me free,

I'll find a new life and maybe a husband or wife.

Love abounds.

So, cut me free or commit to loving me.

Free as a Bird

I'm free as a bird, that's just me.

If I leave tomorrow, forgive me.

There are too many places I've got to see.

So please don't take it personally.

I'm free as a bird, please accept me.

I can't change, so fly with me.

As birds of a feather, we'll fly together.

Free as a bird for all to see.

We'll fly the world together,

Exploring life and finding adventure.

Together we'll fly forever and ever into eternity.

Being free as bird.

Our Time

A woman from the East and a man from the West

Met in a Wisconsin blizzard.

A student teacher and a soldier.

A twenty-four-hour, unexpected travel delay.

Or was it divine intervention?

Monica and Mike.

Love blossomed, uniting two as one.

Love radiated from deep within our hearts and souls.

Marriage united two as one,

Children followed, uniting two as one.

Life's challenges forged our love and devotion,

uniting two as one.

Passing of our daughter united two as one.

Alzheimer's united two as one.

We'll be reunited in heaven, two as one.

We Can't Turn Back Time

We can't turn back time.

One doesn't want to live with past thoughts, tears and regrets.

So, in our final years,

We need to say things that we hold dear.

Now is the time to speak with passion.

For when one of us is gone,

Words remain unheard and unseen.

So, take this time

To speak your heart and mind.

For there be a time when we can't turn back time.

Say the things that lay deep in our hearts

Because there will be a time when we can't turn back time.

The Final Years

Love originates unexpectedly.

A spark goes off.

Or the spark may ignite subsequently.

But a spark must occur to fuel the fire of love.

In the early years of marriage,

There's a yearning to start a family.

Newborns soon arrive.

Mom and Dad sacrifice their relationship to raise offspring.

The spousal bond persists but dependency exists.

The children grow up and leave the nest,

Mom and Dad are left childless.

Travel replaces emptiness.

Living for one another is now pursued.

Retirement arrives along with a social security check.

We can't escape old age.

Taking one another for granted needs to be reassessed.

The Grim Reaper prowls about.

Now's the time your love must be vigorously professed.

Time is ticking much too fast.

Tell each other you love one another multiple times.

Hold and caress one another's hand.

Affectionately touch one another many times.

And don't forget a kiss from time to time.

So, please don't take each other's final years for granted.

Because this may be the last time you'll be together.

When the Flame of Sex Goes Out

We all start out sexless—gender not in doubt,

Running, climbing and hiding about.

As we play, we recognize we're not all alike.

The question arises,

Why is a boy different from a girl?

And why is a girl different from a boy?

Sexuality is now proclaimed.

At first, boys are drawn to girls and girls are curious of boys.

Nothing more exists, until adolescence.

Puberty brings emotional feelings.

Thinking, not acting on feelings.

As young adults, a feeling of sexuality develops.

Possibly an urge to mate without considering the significance.

Love and marriage unites husband and wife.

A family unit is defined.

Procreation may become the purpose of life,

And children arrive.

Thereafter, sex takes on a different role of intimacy.

A bonding of husband and wife throughout their aging life.

As the golden years progress, physical changes take place.

The desire for sex persists

But the physical tools become inept

With the equipment out of service.

The sexual flame that once burned bright

Goes out—but love remains between a husband and wife.

Losses

My best friend

We're born to die,

that's our destiny.

What really matters is what we do in between.

My Lover Gone

My lover is gone

I don't know where I'm going.

I'm blue and feel alone

I just want to be left alone.

My lover is gone

Life rolls on and on.

Somehow, I'll carry on.

The answer to my loss lies within me.

As time passes, I'll feel strong

And I will carry on.

It's hard to believe that once again I'll feel strong,

But life works that way.

So, I must think positive thoughts and be strong today.

I Miss You

I miss you in the wintertime, listening to the rain.

Sitting together by the open fire

And cuddling from time to time.

Sharing coffee as we watch waves crash against the shore.

But most of all, I miss your chatter filling silence in the air.

I miss you in the springtime

When flowers commence to bloom.

Working in the garden in earshot of birds

Twittering springtime tunes,

Sharing sweet springtime fragrances in the air.

But most of all, I miss your aroma that's absent from the air.

I miss you in the summertime when the sun is hot and bright.

At the lake surveying water skiers

Skimming hither and thither about.

Sharing the rickety swing under the pine tree's shade.

But most of all, I miss your comforting stroke and gaze.

I miss you in the autumn, our favorite time of year.

Sharing roadside drives as the leaves turn iridescently bright.

But most of all, I miss your humor and intelligence.

As much as I miss you,

It's comforting to know

we'll be together in the forthcoming years.

The Last Walk

If you should die before me,

a piece of me dies too.

Please walk slowly,

For I want to walk with you.

Stop frequently and look behind,

For I want to walk with you.

Stop and listen for me calling your name,

For I want to walk with you.

When I catch up to you,

Embrace me and take my hand.

We will finish the walk side by side.

So Much for Planning

The greatest disappointment in life

is not spending one's remaining life

With their lifetime lover and partner.

It wasn't supposed to be like this.

We would have celebrated our final years together

For many, many years,

Loving, laughing, conversing, celebrating our togetherness.

It wasn't supposed to be like this.

The love of my life was to live into her nineties.

I was to pass any time after eighty-five.

Our last years were to be the best years.

It wasn't supposed to be like this.

I see my love slowly deteriorate to the innocence of a child

That only Alzheimer's delivers.

She was to be the healthy one, the survivor.

It wasn't supposed to be like this.

I attempt diversion therapy by socializing and joining clubs,

But it's only cosmetic.

As hard as I try to accept the inevitable, I can't let go.

It wasn't supposed to be like this

I love you with my heart and soul.

It wasn't supposed to be like this.

The sun rises, the sun sets.

Night falls and ushers in a new day.

Life goes on.

That's the way it is, no apologies.

It's All Coming Back to Me

My wife is dying of Alzheimer's.

As I watch her drift away,

There are moments in time

When I see flashbacks in time.

I see her as a coed and my bride.

I see her in lingerie lying in bed.

I see her pregnant.

I see her giving birth.

I see our children playing with her.

Things that I could hardly recall are now coming back to me.

I see her camping, fishing, hiking and skiing.

I see her playing slow-pitch and soccer.

I see her gardening.

I see her chauffeuring our children hither and yon.

I see her coming home from work.

It's all coming back to me.

I see her retired.

I see her working out.

I see her traveling with me about.

I see her in Alzheimer's memory care.

When I hear a certain song, it all comes back.

When I touch and kiss her, it all comes back

But I can't see her gone and I can't move on.

which I grudgingly accept.

Final Word

When I've walked my last trail

And traveled my last mile,

Remember me as a person

Who loved his son, daughter, and wife very deeply.

Who accepted the challenge to love mankind.

Who valued his friend's relationships, knowledge, and wisdom.

Who loved nature and believed deeply in God.

Do not forget my faults

For they contributed to my uniqueness.

Remember me when you see a sunrise and a sunset.

Remember me when gazing on the ocean.

Remember me when staring at the stars.

Remember me when feeling the warmth of the sun.

Remember me when looking at Chief Joseph Mountain,

For on that mountain lie my ashes.

Forever I rest in the womb of nature.

My soul lives on in the spirit world.

My body decays and returns to the earth as God intended.

I am at home with my daughter and family.

Life does not end

It just takes a different form.

The soul is eternal.

I'm Halfway Gone

I have Alzheimer's and I'm halfway gone.

Kiss my cheek and caress my hand

For I'm halfway gone.

I'm confused and don't understand.

The best of me is gone.

I need your presence and touch

For I'm halfway gone.

I can't help the way I am.

The disease has taken me on.

The life we shared was glorious and grand.

I'll be leaving you all too soon

For I'm halfway gone.

Please stay beside me,

Take me in your arms.

Love me, kiss me, hold my hand

Until my spark of life is nevermore.

Remember this my darling:

I loved you with my heart and soul.

You were the best partner and lover evermore.

Living Life after the Death of a Loved One

In death there is new life.

I must move forward.

To discover my new life,

I must move forward.

Life doesn't end with death.

Death brings discoveries of a new life.

I must move forward.

Life and death advance mankind.

Life and discoveries are infinite.

I must move forward.

It is up to me

To find new life after death.

I Pass through Heaven's Gate

I enter Heaven's gate,

Home of my ancestors.

My father, mother, wife, and daughter.

I'm an old wise man

Who's made his mark.

I walk tall with much pride.

My daughter stands by the gate.

"Daddy it's been much too long."

She takes my arm as we both walk through Heaven's gate.

My wife appears.

"Dear, I've been eagerly awaiting your arrival."

The three of us walk arm in arm into the spirit world

And beyond.

My mother and father appear.

Dad speaks. "Son I am so proud of you.

You became the man that I never was."

My mother takes me in her arms and says,

"My baby boy is home."

The five of us continue the walk, arm in arm.

Grandpapa appears.

He says, "Peter, you took care of your sisters."

I speak and say,

"Yes, Grandpapa, just as you had commanded."

The six of us continue the walk,

Grandpapa leading the pack.

The whole family clan appears.

Suddenly I feel at home.

The financial competition I felt with father and grandfather

Has passed.

No longer do I feel the need to prove myself.

I am at peace, home at last.

Tomorrow might not come,

and yesterday doesn't really matter that much.

Life's Challenges

Memory care

The Meaning of Life

The world we interpret is relative.

The laws of physics are permanent.

Life's meaning is the above summation.

The Person in the Mirror

When you get what you want,

Your reward may be heartache and tears

If you've fooled the person in the mirror.

Thoughts and Words

Thoughts and words are finite,

How we construct them is infinite.

Their effect is enormous.

A Smile

A frown is an upside-down smile.

A smile draws attention, a frown draws inattention.

A smile lights up a room, a frown dims the room.

A smile sparkles the eyes, a frown dampens the eyes.

A smile removes wrinkles, a frown accentuates wrinkles.

A smile highlights the teeth, a frown hides the teeth.

A smile illuminates the face, a frown clouds over the face.

A smile opens doors, a frown closes doors.

So, which do you choose?

Habits

Do not allow your habits to determine your future.

Your habits limit your opportunities.

Habits and opportunities

And opportunities and habits

Are at constant war.

Self-Fulfilling Prophecy

If you think you can't, it's certain you won't.

If you think you can, it's certain you will.

Your thoughts determine your demeanor.

Your demeanor determines your choices.

Your choices initiate actions.

Your actions launch your future.

Let no circumstances or obstacles inhibit your success.

The individual who wins is the individual who thinks and says,

"I can."

Anything and everything is possible

If you think and say, "I can."

I'm a Simple Man

Are you having a good day?

Yes, I'm having a good day

Because I awoke feeling healthy, happy with a cup of Joe.

Are you having a good day?

Yes, I'm having a good day

Because of the accomplishments that improved my life.

Are you having a good day?

Yes, I'm having a good day

Because of the beauty in nature and life.

Are you having a good day?

Yes, I'm having a good day

Because I have arms, legs, feet and hands.

Are you having a good day?

Yes, I'm having a good day

Because there is a roof over my head,

Food on the table and clothing on my back.

Are you having a good day?

Yes, I'm having a good day

Because I have a fresh start given to me every day.

Are you having a good day?

Yes, I'm having a good day

Because the hard times have made me the person I am today.

Are you having a good day?

Yes, I'm having a good day because I'm self-reliant.

Are you having a good day?

Yes, I'm having a good day because someone smiled at me

And said kind and encouraging words.

Are you having a good day?

Yes, I'm having a good day

Because I have a loving spouse and partner to share life with.

Are you having a good day?

Yes, I'm having a good day

Because I have children, grandchildren and great-grandchildren

To mentor and love.

Are you having a good day?

Yes, I'm having a good day

Because God has given me the wisdom to see

That the simple things in life are all that matter.

Seeds

From day of youth to days old

We contemplate the past to navigate the future.

The seeds we plant sprout the dreams we desire.

Our desires release more seeds to plant.

Soon a plantation appears, giving rise to forest.

Without seeds and dreams, the forest will never appear.

A wasteland without hope and purpose.

Those who dare may fail.

Seeds of failure are the seeds of future success.

Those who fail to dream

Are those who fail to grow.

Imagination is a gift from God.

To perfect oneself is our ordained spiritual purpose.

Lord of Myself

Happiness is found within thee,

A state of mind for all to see.

One doesn't have to have land or money to be happy.

It's appreciating the present, whatever that may be.

We elect to be happy or unhappy,

Created by the circumstances affecting thee.

Pleasant circumstances are obviously pleasing and gratifying.

Unpleasant circumstances require a choice.

Will I allow the circumstance to make me unhappy?

Unhappy thoughts generate unhappiness.

Unhappiness generates hopelessness.

Hopelessness generates more unhappy thoughts

And unhappiness.

To find happiness in an unpleasant circumstance,

Accept the distasteful incident,

Find the silver lining—every negative has a positive outcome.

Focus and exploit the positive consequence.

One's happiness has nothing to do with one's character.

It's all about one's state of mind.

Change your thinking and happiness is magnified.

Down but Not Out

Life is unpredictable and filled with risk.

Remember this, you may be down but not out.

Pick yourself up, dust yourself off and move on.

You've been there before, turning your failure about.

You may be down but not out.

Don't Quit.

You're down on your knees, all can see.

Stand up tall and pipedream big.

You may be down but not out.

Don't Quit.

You've been kicked in the head

By those aspiring to keep you down.

Ignore the discouragement and pain.

Retort "You haven't seen the last of me yet."

Don't Quit.

You've been told you couldn't do this or that

Or weren't astute enough.

Success is failure turned inside-out.

Don't Quit.

Listen to your heart, follow your dreams.

Believe in yourself.

Never give up.

Don't Quit.

Look in the mirror for clarity.

Keep your prospective sincere.

Nothing will stop you achieving success.

If you Don't Quit.

Living Life to the Fullest

The greatest gift is life.

How you live life is up to thee.

Do I choose safety and security?

Do I take risks and live adventurously?

The answer lies in our hearts.

You must listen to thee.

Your heart will speak freely.

To live is to risk dying.

To hope is to risk despair.

To try is to risk failure.

To love is to risk rejection.

Risk must be taken.

The greatest risk is to not to take risk.

Those who risk nothing,

Do nothing, have nothing, are nothing, and become nothing.

Those who take risks grow, love, and are truly free.

Living life to the fullest.

✧✧✧

Loneliness

As the sun rises, the earth warms.

The fog of loneliness blows in, surrounding the senses.

Overwhelming the cognitive.

Resulting in self-imposed solitude.

As the sun rises higher, the fog retreats.

Loneliness evaporates, solitude remains.

Loneliness return at dusk.

Night captures the cognitive.

Self-imposed solitude continues.

The wind ushers in wholeness of mind.

Accept the past, embrace the future.

Participate in life's activities.

Loneliness and solitude disappear.

From teachings and cultures of old,

I've learned the woman's role.

I give of myself knowingly so,

To please and serve others to make me whole.

Lovingly I fulfill my role.

Life events changed my role.

My partner of old has asked me to go.

I feel lost to the depth of my soul.

Forgiveness has no role.

I thought I knew the woman's role.

My children must know

Mom will continue as old.

I reach down into my soul and find the strength

Only a woman knows.

I raise my children to know there is no woman's role.

I've learned the woman's role,

independence is my goal.

I've made a new life for all to know.

I love my life and all men must know.

Never again will I please others to make me whole.

Insecurities

Insecurity lies within us all.

Insecurity is self-doubt.

Self-doubt is fear.

Fear is not knowing the unknown.

The unknown is all about.

To live life is to experience fear.

Fearing life is not living life

For life is full of fears.

Insecurities and self-doubt are no more than self-lies.

To deal with fear, one must set insecurities aside.

To set insecurities aside,

One must accept fears as a fact of life.

To deal with insecurities, make a plan.

Self-discipline now comes to hand.

For without self-discipline, the plan can't be carried out.

And lack of performance, brings back self-doubt.

Insecurities then return.

There's no way out other than going straight ahead.

The plan and discipline must be achieved.

So, get back in the boat and row like hell.

Peace of mind comes with moving on.

Remember this: insecurities are more likely unreal.

Misfortune or Opportunity

The sun rises, the sun sets.

The sun sets, the sun rises.

Life begins anew.

The past is the past.

The future is the future.

The choices we make every day

Inaugurate sadness or happiness.

Our state of mind is a choice.

Change your brain, change your life.

If the glass is half empty,

The forecast looks doubtful with clouds and rain.

If the glass is half full,

The sun is out, and the forecast looks bright and shiny.

Sadness and despair are found in the half-empty glass.

Happiness and joy are found in the half-full glass.

Misfortune and bad luck are found in the glass half empty.

Opportunities are found in the glass half full.

Misfortune and bad luck need to be spun into opportunities.

Life goes on and on and on.

Misfortune and opportunities occur every twenty-four hours.

We choose whether the glass is half empty or half full.

Family

When I was very young,

Mom and Dad provided constraint, security and love.

The security and love were okay,

But not the constraints, so I say.

As a newlywed,

The family comprised my spouse and me.

Loyalty, devotion and commitment to fidelity.

Children soon arrived.

The family took on a new sense of worth and pride.

Loving, mentoring, nurturing,

And teaching honesty and morality.

Too quickly, the children grew up and left home.

Living in places far away from home.

The family embodied my spouse and me, our children afar.

Suddenly the focus was back on us.

When grandchildren arrived,

The family increased in size.

Fixating on the little ones underfoot.

Loving, mentoring, nurturing.

Teaching honesty and morality,

Grandpa and Grandma so taught.

When the grandchildren had children,

The family was aptly large and not always in touch.

Kinship and bloodline became the yoke.

But stories, lessons and values

Taught by Great-Grandpa and Grandma were memorialized.

And the circle of family values and history was kept alive.

Obesity

Three meals a day keeps the hunger at bay.

Mid-morning, mid-afternoon and late-night snacks

Are not lacking.

Obviously, I overeat.

My job and family causes stress.

Meals to prepare, youngsters to chauffeur hither and yon.

The daily grind plays on.

I'm not addicted to food—it just comforts me.

My health is important, but I can't find time for me.

I would love to be slender and fit.

But giving to other requires entirely all my commitment.

Nothing is more satisfying than sweets at any time.

I huff and I puff when walking to work.

But my reward is a donut afterwards.

The bathroom scale is terribly unkind.

The mirror reflects flab beyond my reminiscence.

I don't recognize the person I am.

That's it! I'm sick of it!

I'm tired of focusing on others at my deficit.

It's time to overhaul me.

My health is of utmost eminence.

I can't continue using food to placate myself.

No longer will I be enthralled by unhealthy eats.

Exercise and healthy eating is a lifestyle I must accept.

My spouse, children and employees are depending on me

And my poor health is preempting me.

So, it's fish, chicken and two meats a week.

Vegetables and fruits, all I can eat.

I go to the gym twofold a week,

And walk in the morning to accelerate my metabolic rate.

I'm losing weight but no one can see.

Oh well—it's all about me.

Then suddenly people ask me,

"Are you losing weight?"

It's now clear for all to see.

I've lost one-hundred-plus pounds over several years.

My blood sugar, blood pressure and cholesterol

Have dropped significantly.

I'm healthy and plan on continuing that way.

Unhealthy food no longer tempt me.

HOORAY! I'm healthy and all can see.

My Aging Breasts

I've had my breasts from birth.

Small brown dots at first.

During pubescence, they grew a lot.

Not too little, not a lot.

My cleavage was really hot.

When babies arrived, a new episode of my life embarked.

My breasts were used for nursing.

For many years thereafter, my breasts retained their form.

Then breast cancer came unannounced,

A double mastectomy was announced.

The night before the surgery, I hugged them

And cried out, "We've had a good life, my bosom dear."

The cancer was removed along with my breasts.

And I grieved the loss of my breasts.

I now have two new artificial breasts.

Hooray for me, "I'm cancer free!"

Rejoicing and giving thanks.

For those who survived breast cancer, remember this:

Loved ones could care less about your breasts.

It's only you who recalls the breasts.

Down Syndrome

I've had Down syndrome from birth.

Down syndrome is a condition, not a disease.

I don't suffer from it, nor do I feel impaired.

I'm happy being me.

I have forty-seven chromosomes

As opposed to forty-six in thee.

Just like you my, chromosomes define me.

I may look different than thee,

But the differences delineate me.

I'm short, have broad facial features, and am loving.

I feel the same emotions as thee.

I like interacting with people socially.

Acknowledge me so I'm comfortable integrating socially.

I have a unique personality and interests just like thee.

I can be an athlete, musician, artist, and join clubs with thee.

Having fun and friends is important to me.

Living a normal life is very important to me.

I have feelings just like thee.

I feel hurt and upset when someone is mean to me.

It's **not** ok to use the word "retard" to describe me.

Retard does not define or describe me,

For I'm as normal as I can be.

I'm unique and it's obvious to see.

I can be whatever GOD intended for me.

I can compensate for my inabilities.

Help me be whatever I dream to be.

Love me.

Witnessing Alzheimer's

Witnessing Alzheimer's is like

Watching a bonfire slowly burn down to embers.

Amid a thousand days and nights

Mourning the loss

Up and until the embers die out.

Out of the lair of their environment

Come the victims of their surroundings and teachings.

The innocents of ignorance

The young, middle-aged, and old.

The children of:

Unwanted mothers and fathers,

Poverty,

Drug addiction and mental illness,

Physical and sexual abuse.

The middle-aged:

Uneducated and unskilled,

Tools of commerce-seeking profit,

Slaves of minimum wage.

The old:

Broken-down bodies,

Cast-offs of capitalism.

Living:

On sidewalks and vacant land,

In parks, culverts, and thresholds.

Scorned by society.

Hopeless, with no direction.

Our brothers and sisters.

There but for the grace of GOD, go I.

Give not compassion.

Do not give a handout—offer a hand up.

Give inspiration, hope, and love.

Offer:

Drug and mental health treatment

Conditional housing

Counseling

Bridge to education and trades.

There but for the grace of GOD, go I.

God within Thee

Deep inside our brain

Lies a spiritual side of thee.

Scientists call it the "God spot."

The name doesn't matter for GOD resides within thee.

To connect to GOD within thee,

One must first believe there's a GOD who oversees thee.

One must cry aloud, "GOD I love you with my heart and soul."

One must praise GOD

And commit to the destiny planned for thee.

Do not pray for things you control.

Pray for wisdom, strength, and healing.

Ask GOD for forgiveness for shameful things you've done.

Tell GOD you will accept and follow the intended plan for thee.

Tell GOD you'll help yourself.

For GOD will not help you unless you help thee.

Then never give up on your prayer,

GOD will respond.

The journey may be strange,

But keep believing

and GOD will show you the way.

Money Poems

Mom and son – Life is good

Money, Money, Money

If I had money, the things I could do.

The opposite sex would find me engaging, attractive,

And loveable too.

I could buy expensive possessions and be well-to-do.

I would travel the world with no toil to do.

I'd be able to invest in stocks and be philanthropist too.

Oh, the things I could do.

Guess what? I just won the lottery!

I'm rich and all will soon know.

I quit my job and bought a big house.

Spend, spend, spend is now what I do.

I left my wife for a younger woman with beauty possessed.

I bought a Mercedes, boat, and a motor coach.

I now travel the world with my lady anew.

Spending my wealth is the fun thing for us to do.

Guess what? I'm now broke with nothing to show.

And my lady of new is gone too.

I was a fool.

I've learned a hard lesson.

Money doesn't bring happiness.

So, if I ever have a windfall of money once again,

I'll spend the money on meaningful things.

Like family, relationships, self-improvement,

And assisting others in need.

A hard lesson well learned.

The Gold Digger's Prey

Twenty years my junior, blond hair, big boobs

And eyes of blue.

I'm so lucky to meet a lady like you.

You ask me if I love you.

Being a rich man, I'll prove my love to you.

I'll buy you jewels, fur coats and a BMW.

I'll build a gated mansion on a mountaintop.

And if that's not enough, here's what I'll do.

I'll buy a Nordstrom department store,

So you can clandestinely shop.

That's how much I love you.

Do you love me?

> Yes, my darling, I love you, you're the best.
>
> I'll snuggle, cuddle and hold your hand.
>
> I'll make love to you like no one can.
>
> Eight o'clock every night, I'll tuck you in bed,
>
> Kissing you goodnight.
>
> I'll never leave you, for I'll be there when you expire.

And all I ask for in your best interest is for power of attorney,

So I can assist in managing your affairs.

I'm so lucky to have a beautiful and loving lady like you.

My family says your love is untrue.

Don't listen to your family, listen to me.

If you give me power of attorney, I'll care for your family.

Trust my love in thee.

Ok, I'll trust in thee. Please take care of my family!

I promise to care for your family.

But who's going to care for me?

I'll care for you, what's the cost?

I suggest we set up a living trust.

Okay, that makes sense, I love you, my dear.

And darling, I love you too.

Another foolish old man falls prey to the gold digger's dance.

Does Money Make You Happy?

Does money make you happy?

The simple answer is maybe.

Money in itself doesn't make you happy.

Happiness comes from within.

But the way you spend money can make you happy.

Spending discretionary money on

Relationships:

Visiting family and friends,

Attending social and family events,

Gifting.

Experiences:

Travel, especially with family and friends,

Experiences with grandchildren,

Activities cultivating relationships.

Things of interest:

Self-improvement, education, and hobbies.

Discipline:

Diets, exercise, pets, and self-improvement classes.

Stress relief:

Therapists, counselors, maids, gardeners.

Don't spend money on alcohol or drugs

For they will not make you happy.

Financial peace of mind:

Debt reduction and savings.

Helping others:

Charities and giving others in need a helping hand.

If you have a problem that money can solve,

You have no problem.

Money is not evil,

It's the love of money that's evil.

When the stock market is low, you buy.

When the stock market is high, you sell.

Be a contrarian.

What the wise man does in the beginning,

The fool does in the end.

Selling your winning companies

And adding to your bad companies

Is like watering weeds.

Hold, add to and water the winning companies.

Option Trading

Option trading is a dance with Lady Luck.

You have a forty percent probability of success, or maybe less.

Option trading can be happy-hour talk.

If you use a *call* to sell a stock,

Look out for falling market explosiveness.

If you need a *put* to protect a stock,

You shouldn't buy the stock.

Buying and selling *straddles* and *strangles*

And *going naked* is throwing the dice.

To be successful, you need insider advice.

Inside advice may incarcerate you for an extended time.

Credit and debit spreads sometime work nice.

The key term is *sometimes* they work nice.

Advance option trading strategies

Are the playgrounds of the pros.

Venturing outside your experience and skills

May result in the entire portfolio collapsing about.

So, when you hear idle stock option talk,

Remember this: the money is made

Leveraging option premiums, not stocks.

And paying too much for option premiums

Can put you in hock.

Stay safe with covered calls, puts and stocks.

[This poem summarizes my experience with option trading. I bless covered calls and puts. All other option trading strategies require the use of option trading computer software and implementation of the Greeks.]

Story Poems

Mom and son

My Best Friend Me

My best friend, Me, is easy to please.

We never argue, we always agree.

Me likes the same things as we.

What a wonderful friend I have in Me.

One day, Me said he didn't like me.

"You are too conceited," said Me.

"I'm not conceited," I said to Me.

"I just have excessive pride in myself."

"Oh yes, you are conceited," said Me.

"I don't like egos or conceit," I told Me.

"Then change your ways," said Me.

"How do I change?" I asked.

"Don't be egotistical or a know-it-all," said Me.

"I love myself," I told Me, "I'm so clever, can't you see?"

"You're not clever at all," said Me.

"Your ego is overwhelming.

The only help I can offer," said Me,

"is to look into the mirror and listen to thee.

Quit talking, listen to others," said Me.

I've taken the advice of Me.

I now have many more friends than previously.

I'm Losing My Hair

I'm losing my hair with much despair.

Despair means no hope for hair.

It's disappearing, there's nothing more I can say.

As a young man,

My hair was short and fair.

I sported a flat top.

An athletic look was vogueish and hip.

The Beatles landed in 1965.

My hair was brown and long then.

I wore a Prince Valiant hairstyle and it was kool.

Disco era came along.

We danced to the tune "Stayin' Alive."

Prince Valiant hairstyle was still going strong.

My hair remained long.

Short hair made a comeback in 1995.

Then I was middle-aged and beginning to gray.

I wore short hair with a part on the side.

My hairline sustained, I was peppered with gray.

Ten years then passed,

My hairline remained robust.

But my hair went snowy white.

I was a still a good-looking man, the ladies would say.

So, my ego remained in play.

When I claimed Social Security

I looked in the mirror.

My hair was receding and thinning from the front to the rear.

My hairline and color defined my good looks.

But I was transforming to a new look.

Soon I would be without hair.

NO HAIR!!!

A catastrophe was declared.

I talked to my doctor, who prescribed Rogaine.

So I rubbed Rogaine into my hair, morning and night.

It made my hair sticky and stiff white.

I didn't look right.

So, I threw in the towel, accepting the passing of my hair.

To this day, I fondly remember my hair.

What more can I say?

Hey, it happens that way.

Beautiful Feet

Without a doubt, I have beautiful feet.

Twenty-six bones and thirty-three joints compose my foot.

The tibia and fibula shape my ankle joint forming my heel,

The strongest bone in my foot.

The midfoot is a miracle of engineering,

Providing both flexibility and strength.

But my favorite of all is the forefoot.

Five toes each, ten in all,

Connected by five metatarsal bones and five shorter bones.

What I love about my feet is mobility.

I can walk, run, climb and pick up objects with my toes.

Most of all, I relish my toes.

Toes are well ordered, kool and very neat.

I like wiggling my toes and watching them flex.

Fashioning toenails into different shapes.

Filing the tips smooth and white

And coloring the nails with pretty colors of paint.

I feel so sexy when I procure a pedicure.

Fifteen different types of pedicures

Render my feet charming and picturesque.

I usually get a French pedicure with toenail tips snowy white.

When I feel whimsical,

I'll order an ice cream pedicure flavor of my choice.

There's no pedicure I dislike.

Pedicurist soaks and messages my feet.

Pumice stone removes calluses on the bottom of my feet.

The toenails are cut to form and filed to shape.

Attention to details is what like.

Today I'm purchasing a gel pedicure

Painted iridescently bright.

Several coats of nail polish are applied.

Each coat is exposed to UV light.

After three coats, my nails are dry

Yet look conspicuously wet and bright.

I love my toes and pedicures.

For I truly have the most beautiful feet.

Big Voodoo Daddy

In 1619, the first slave ship arrived in Jamestown.

Big Voodoo Daddy was one of twenty slaves who disembarked.

The name "Big Daddy" was consigned.

A mountain of a man at six foot six.

A figure of strength and ferocious independence.

Shackled from neck to toe.

Big Daddy went to market.

Bidding commenced.

Six hundred, seven hundred, one thousand, twelve hundred,

Big Daddy was sold.

Led off naked in chains, Big Daddy wasn't afraid.

Chained to horse-drawn wagon,

Big Daddy walked a fifth of a fortnight and then

Arrived at a plantation.

Housed in a shanty with six slave mates,

Big Daddy worked the fields during the daylight.

At night, Big Daddy was bred again and again.

Never to know his offspring or kin.

Seven days a week, fourteen hours a day,

Big Daddy labored as an obedient slave.

Son of an African chief, Big Daddy never masked his pride.

The slave keepers beat Big Daddy once a day.

And failed to compromise Big Daddy's pride.

His owner shopped Big Daddy, at any price.

Sold for three-quarters of his original price.

Big Daddy worked the master's house,

A striking figure in formal attire.

The master paid Big Daddy a buck fifty a week

After many years, Big Daddy secured his sovereignty.

Big Daddy worked the master's house for five more years,

Purchasing passage to Africa where he backtracked.

After thirty-plus years,

Big Voodoo Daddy returned to his tribe.

His mother had died, his father still chief.

Unification occurred like no one had ever seen.

The village cried, wailed, and danced way into the night.

His father removed his crown,

Placed the crown on his son's head.

Big Voodoo Daddy was officially crowned

Chief of the Zulu clan.

The Big, Brown Bear

A big, brown bear came after me out of nowhere,

I didn't stand a chance.

So, we danced and danced and danced

The bear made the final offensive advance.

As I lay on the ground facedown,

I wrapped my arms tightly around the back of my neck

And lay very still.

As the bear stood over me, I could smell its rancid breath.

The bear attempted to get its mouth around my neck.

I wouldn't release my grip protecting my neck.

I fought to stay on my belly

As the bear endeavored to flip me over to finish me off.

I felt no pain as the bear bit me time after time,

Again and again.

Blood was running into my eyes and I was partially blind.

Finally, the bear moved away,

And I barely saw two cubs scampering about.

The cubs moved forward, sniffing the air.

I didn't move a muscle, lying motionless—but I wasn't scared.

Mama bear made one last charge then sauntered away.

I lay on the ground thinking *I don't want to die!*

I fell asleep and my wife and children materialized.

"Daddy, I love you, please don't die," my daughters cried.

I felt a warm wet cloth on the back of my hands,

Still protecting my neck.

Voices shouted out, "Fido come here,"

Then two hikers appeared.

I lay on the ground helpless and near death.

But I remembered my wife and children who had appeared.

I cried out loudly and said,

"I won't die, I have two children to raise."

Just like the big, brown bear.

A Gypsy with Wings

Florica Lyubs was her name, a Romanian Gypsy.

Her Romanian name in English translated to Flower Love.

Florica was born in a horse-drawn wagon.

Her papa worked for anyone, doing whatever he could.

Her mama danced for money.

Florica didn't go to school.

She learned the wrong lessons from Mama and Papa,

Ending up in trouble a lot.

At sixteen she took up dancing.

Florica and Mama would dance to please men.

Florica soon became known as the dancing Gypsy.

Florica had a talent that no one knew.

She had a singing voice that would open gates.

One night, as she danced about, she sang aloud.

A songwriter was watching her dance.

The song she sang brought the writer to tears.

Florica hit every note.

The songwriter knew Florica was predestined to sing his songs.

She was shy, and when he asked her to sing his songs,

Trusting men wasn't for her.

The songwriter returned night after night,

Pleading with Florica to sing the songs he'd written.

Finally, Florica agreed.

Her first published song was "Gypsy."

The song went right to the top of the charts.

Florica knew she no longer had to dance for men.

Florica became the top European female vocalist of all time.

She never forgot her past.

She gave thanks to GOD every day and gifted her money away.

She established the Florica Lyubs Gypsy Academic and
    Performing Arts Institute,

Providing a helping hand to underprivileged children.

Her farewell and the last song she sang was

"You Can Be Whatever You Dream."

Her tombstone reads, "A Gypsy with Wings."

Wiley Wallaby

Wiley Wallaby lived in the bush among many trees.

Wiley's troupe was made up of boomers.

Jill, a female wallaby,

Lived in the neighboring bush adjacent to Wiley.

Wiley enjoyed watching Jill hopping to and fro.

Jill was so engaging, browsing among the bushes and trees.

Wiley adore the female wallaby.

Jill wanted a buck to start a family.

Wiley courted Jill in the bushes and under the trees.

Jill accepted Wiley.

Jill gave birth to a baby male joey.

Wiley thereafter joined a court of mature male wallabies.

Jill was left to raise and provide for her joey.

Single mom was Jill's destiny.

Her baby joey hunkered down in mom's pouch.

Six months later, came out with a bounce.

Hopping free wasn't to be.

Joey needed warmth and milk to flourish

Midst the bushes and trees.

So, Joey frequently returned to mother's pouch.

Another six months passed. and mom's pouch wasn't to last.

One day when Joey was hopping about,

Mom closed her pouch.

Joey returned to find out

He no longer resided in mom's pouch.

Joey was frantic, hopping about.

"Where is my pouch?" the young Joey gasped.

Jill stayed steadfast,

No pouch for Joey to grasp.

Joey moved on to meet other bucks.

He soon joined a troupe of jacks.

The young Joey soon found his Jill,

And his life began at last.

[A wallaby is a small to mid-sized macropod native to Australia and New Guinea. Another early name for the wallaby, in use from at least 1802, was the brush-kangaroo. They belong to the same family as kangaroos. Eleven species of brush wallabies exist. Young wallabies are known as joeys, like many other marsupials. Adult male wallabies are referred to as bucks, boomers, or jacks. An adult female wallaby is known as a doe, flyer, or jill. A group of wallabies is called a court, mob, or troupe. – https://en.wikipedia.org/wiki/wallaby]

Personal Favorites

The entire family

Who Do I Promote?

"One person with passion is greater than

the passive force of ninety-nine who have only an interest."

John L. Mason

The LORD is my shepherd; I shall not want.

He maketh me to lie down in green pastures: he leadeth me beside the still waters.

He restoreth my soul: he leadeth me in the paths of righteousness for his name's sake.

Yea, though I walk through the valley of the shadow of death, I will fear no evil: for thou art with me; thy rod and thy staff they comfort me.

Thou preparest a table before me in the presence of mine enemies: thou anointest my head with oil; my cup runneth over.

Surely goodness and mercy shall follow me all the days of my life: and I will dwell in the house of the LORD for ever.

Holy Bible

Alzheimer's Wish

Do not ask me to remember

Don't try to make me understand

Let me rest and know you're with me

Kiss my cheek and hold my hand.

I'm confused beyond your concept

I am sad and sick and lost

All I know is that I need you

to be with me at all cost.

Do not lose your patience with me

Do not scold or curse or cry

I can't help the way I'm acting

Can't be different though I try.

Just remember that I need you,

That the best of me is gone

Please don't fail to stand beside me

Love me 'til my life is done.

Owen Darnell

Mike's wife, Monica, had Alzheimer's and was in a memory care facility during the course of publishing this book. Poetry became the tool Mike used to deal with the long, emotional goodbye to his wife of fifty years. His mental health hinged on his ability to put life's experiences in perspective. Mike's first poems were written to Monica and dealt with love and grief. His poetry further developed into pieces about life experiences and inspirational stories. Mike's purpose in writing poetry was to capture the emotional events that all people encounter in some form or another but perhaps with a different spin on the outcome.

Mike was born in Seattle, Washington, attended Queen Anne High School, Everett Community College, and Seattle University. Mike graduated from Seattle University with a Bachelor of Arts in business, a major in accounting, and a second lieutenant commission in the U.S. Army. Mike served in Vietnam as a forward observer supporting infantry operations for one year.

Upon being discharged from active military duty, Mike drove from Fort Dix, New Jersey, to Seattle, Washington. Along the way, he was stranded in a gas station and restaurant in Rothsay, Minnesota during a blizzard. There, Mike met Monica—a beautiful and charming college girl—who later became his wife. After seven years in Vancouver, Mike and Monica moved to Olympia, Washington. Mike's passions, outside of his work, include his family, hiking, biking, skiing, and fishing.

If my poetry collection provided some insight and comfort for you, please write a review and share your thoughts so others may also experience the same benefits.

Thank you,

Mike